*The One Thing*

# The One Thing

MATTHEW KELLY

Beacon
PUBLISHING

*Photo Credits:*

FRONT COVER AND PAGES 6, 11, 15, 17, 18, 30-31, 38, 42, 50,
52-53, 57 : MATTHEW KELLY
BACK COVER: ELLIE BURKE
PAGES 8-9: OUR 365 STUDIOS
PAGES 12-13, 22-23, 24, 26, 28, 32, 41, 47, 49, 55, 58:
MEGGIE BURKE
PAGES 34-35: ROB ROECKNER / OUR 365 STUDIOS
PAGE 37 : MARY JO BURKE
PAGE 44: KATHY AULL
PAGE 61: HELEN ADAMS

Published by BEACON PUBLISHING.

ISBN: 978-0-9841318-8-4

Printed in the United States.

For more information visit: www.DynamicCatholic.com

FIRST EDITION

*Book Design by Shawna Powell*

*For*

*Walter Patrick Kelly*

Last night my son woke in the middle of the night crying. His name is Walter Patrick, and he is our first child. Now just ten months old, he has brought more joy to my life than I ever thought I would experience, and I have discovered that I am capable of a love that amazes me almost on a daily basis.

I went to his room and, taking him from his crib, placed him on my shoulder. He was immediately soothed. A minute later I could have put him back in his crib and no doubt he would have slept

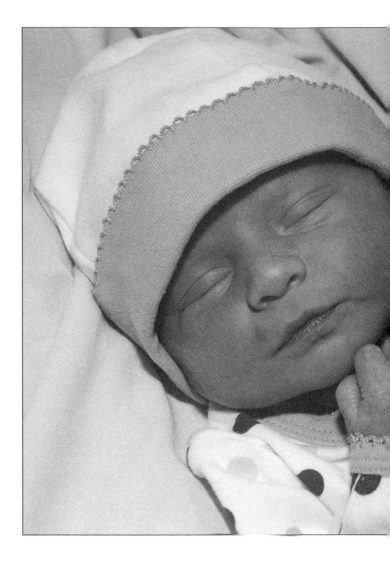

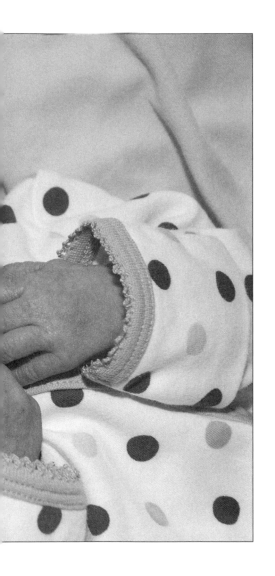

peacefully for the rest of the night. But I cherish these moments with him. I like to hold him as he sleeps on my shoulder, nuzzling his face into my neck, and I think about the life he will lead.

I wonder what life will hold for him—what his interests will be, what he will do professionally, what the great challenges and passions of his life will be, and mostly, how he will develop into the man he was born to become. These thoughts always lead me to prayer. Sometimes I pray the ancient prayers of Christianity, and sometimes I just spontaneously call out to God, asking him to bless my son and watch over him. Often my eyes fill with tears. They are the tears of a very happy man who finds himself contented in a quite unexpected way, and before long I find myself immersed in a sea of gratitude.

I sat there last night holding Walter longer

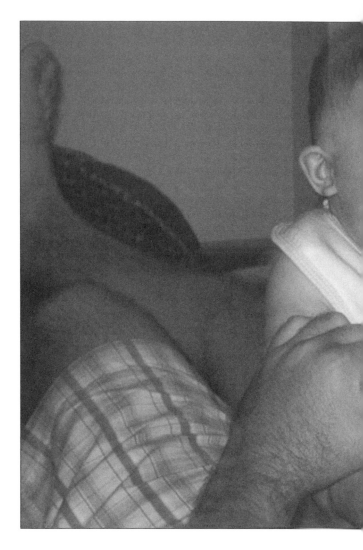

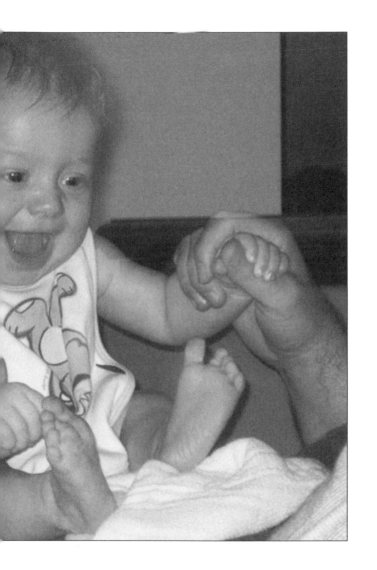

than usual, and, in the midst of my thoughts and prayers, I was filled with questions. They were questions about passing faith onto children: Will my son grow to appreciate the Catholic faith the way I do? Will he attend church joyfully? Will he go through a rebellious stage? Will he reject the faith of his parents and leave the Catholic Church? Will he be attracted to another religion? Will the secularism of today's culture turn him away from organized religion altogether?

All this wondering got me thinking about how I will speak to my son about spirituality, religion, and God. And so, I began to reflect on why a life of faith is so important to me.

My life has been remarkably blessed. I suspect I have experienced more joy than most, and while there have certainly been dark moments in my journey, I have not suffered anywhere near as

much as some. But I do witness human suffering in all its forms. Sometimes it is the result of an accident, and at other times it is the aftermath of a natural disaster. However, it seems to me that the great majority of suffering people experience in this world is because we don't live up to the great human commission. This commission consists simply of being human. It is when we are less than human that we bring suffering upon others. Animals are not capable of patience, compassion, generosity, or any of the greatness that is uniquely human.

Religion is the primary humanizing force in a person, in a society, in history. In my own experience this is particularly true of the Catholic form of Christianity. Catholicism makes me a-better-version-of-myself. It makes me more human.

It is when we begin to lose a grip on our hu-

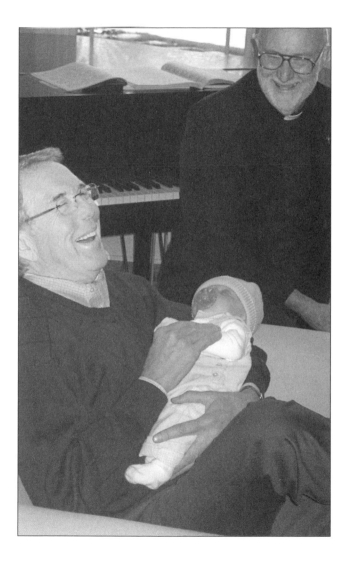

manity that the long betrayal of self begins. This betrayal always ends with us turning our backs on God, hurting other people, and engaging in some form of self-destruction. It is by running toward God that we run toward our true selves. It is our faith that empowers us to walk with God by loving the people who cross our paths and celebrating our best selves. And yes, this is something I want for my son.

Do I want my son to grow up and embrace the Catholic faith? Yes. I suppose all parents who take the spiritual life seriously want to pass on their particular religious tradition to their children. But I don't want him to stay out of compulsion or guilt, and I certainly don't want him to stay to please his mother or me. I would like my son to immerse himself in the Catholic faith because somewhere deep within it resonates with him, speaks to him, moves him.

Albert Einstein wrote, "I want to know the thoughts of God. Everything else is details." I hope my son develops an intimate friendship with God, a curiosity about the Divine, an appreciation for all things spiritual, and an understanding of Jesus Christ - the turning point of human history.

In all my life I don't think I have held such a lofty ambition as that of passing the faith onto my children. How will it be achieved? What can I do to bring it to fruition? Is it within my influence or beyond it?

And while I ponder these questions, I know it is impossible to ignore the unprecedented exodus taking place at this time as men and woman of all ages leave the Catholic Church. Where do they go? Some are drawn to the allure of nondenominational megachurches. Many just stop going to church altogether. Why do they leave? I suspect it is a combination of factors. Even the most casual observer would conclude that two of those factors seem to be that they don't know what they are leaving and that the Church failed to speak into their lives in a way compelling enough to engage them.

Will I be able to instruct my son adequately about the beauty and genius of Catholicism? Will the Church learn to speak directly to the triumphs and trials, the questions and concerns of his life? I hope so.

What began as a passing thought very quickly became a complex web of fears, hopes, and anxieties. I have made a life by simplifying the complex, so I sought simplicity. I thought to myself, if I could teach my son one thing that would

ensure his appreciation of Catholicism, what would it be? What's the one thing?

I looked at the clock. I had been sitting there holding my beautiful boy for almost two hours. But I couldn't put him down. He was sleeping soundly, and my mind was working its way through these questions.

I thought about people I know who have left the Catholic Church and others who have given up on religion altogether. I thought about the thousands of parents who have lamented to me about their children leaving the Church. It was then that I stumbled on a question that made me uneasy. What would it take for Matthew Kelly to leave the Catholic Church?

For a long time I sat there combing through the lowest moments in Catholic history, testing each to see if one of them would have been the

breaking point that made me leave. After thinking it through, I couldn't find sufficient reason in any of those moments to leave the Church. Instead, what I found were examples of what happens when people don't live the Catholic faith authentically. I found immorality and personal weakness, psychopathic selfishness and the abuse of power. I found Christ's teaching misunderstood and misrepresented. But the scandals that stain our history do not exist because we lived our Catholicism, but rather, because we failed to live it. And what I found most of all in the Church's history was a reflection of my own fragile and broken humanity.

So, what would have to happen for me to leave the Catholic Church? I can't imagine anything that would bring me to that point. Yes, I have been disappointed by some of the things people

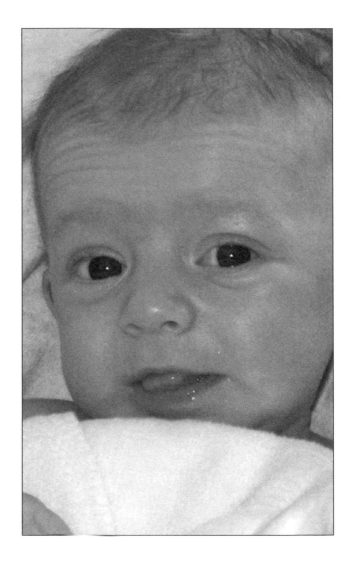

who claim to be Catholic do, I wish our leaders were bold and decisive, I think the Church needs overwhelming renewal, but I don't think I could ever leave the Church. The reason is because I believe that Jesus Christ is alive in the Eucharist. And no protestant, evangelical, or nondenominational church can give me that.

My parish is by no means the most dynamic faith community in the world. If I went looking, I am certain I could find better music. I suspect I would not have to search far to find a better homily. I could even find a more vibrant faith community. And as Catholics we should work tirelessly to improve the quality of all of these. But none of these compares with being able to receive the body and blood of Christ in the Eucharist.

You see, I can come to Mass on Sunday and the homily can be a disaster, the music can be a

train wreck, and there can be kids running up and down the aisles throwing their crayons and eating snacks. But the moment when I receive the Eucharist is a pivotal moment in my week. It's a moment of transformation, a moment where I get to receive who and what I wish to become. And I cannot leave that. It wouldn't matter how good the music or preaching was elsewhere, I cannot leave the Eucharist. I cannot leave Jesus.

And so, sitting there with my son, I discovered that one thing I could teach him to ensure his appreciation of Catholicism: I could teach my son to appreciate the true presence of Jesus in the Eucharist. For it is the belief that Jesus is truly present in the Eucharist—not just symbolically so—that seems to be one of the key differences between highly engaged Catholics and those who walk away from the Church. It may be *the* difference.

---

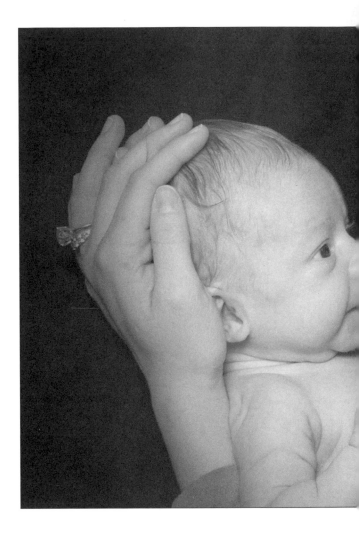

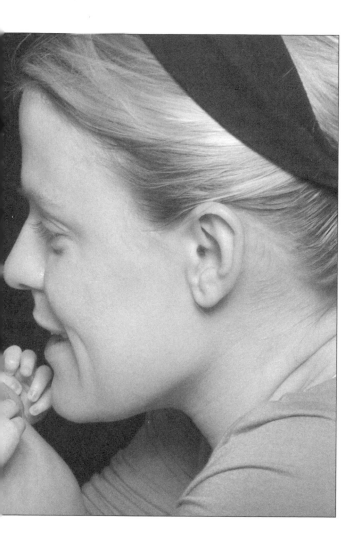

Interestingly, for all the people who have left the Catholic Church over the years, I don't know a single person who has left who believes in the true presence. It is what sets the Catholic Church apart from all modern forms of Christianity.

If I reflect upon the gift of faith that I have been given, I am led to the conclusion that once we believe in the Eucharist we are given the grace to look beyond a bad homily and the grace to look beyond a good homily, the grace to look beyond uninspiring music and the grace to look beyond music that elevates our hearts, minds, and souls. For it is beyond all these things that we find Jesus in the Eucharist.

Of course, it is not an easy teaching to believe. It is the most controversial issue in Christian history, and from the very beginning people had trouble believing it. Jesus said, "I am the

bread of life. . . . Unless you eat the flesh of the Son of Man and drink his blood, you have no life in you. Whoever eats my flesh and drinks my blood has eternal life, and I will raise them up on the last day."

How did the people of his time react to this teaching? "On hearing it, many of his disciples said, 'This is a hard teaching, who can accept it?'" Isn't that exactly what so many people say now, two thousand years later?

And what did many of Jesus' followers do in response to this teaching? We are told in John's Gospel, "From this time many of his disciples turned back and no longer followed him." And so it has been in every place and time since that day. Many people turn their back on Catholicism to-day because they are unable to believe in the true presence.

What did Jesus say to the twelve, and what does he say to you and me today? "Do you want to leave too?" How will you answer him? How will my son Walter answer him? And his children, my grandchildren a generation away yet, how will they answer?

Peter's reply was this, "Lord, to whom would we go? You have the words of eternal life" (John 6:35–68). Not only does Jesus have the words of eternal life, he is the bread of life. It is the bread of life that I yearn for, it's this bread that sustains me, it's the bread that allows me to continue little by little to overcome the weaknesses of my character and to become a-better-version-of-myself. So I will never leave the Church, and I will never leave because I believe in the true presence.

The Scriptures are full of references to the Eucharist, but many people find the leap from

these words to the reality of the true presence too daunting. Nonetheless, if you have doubts or disbelief, set them aside for a moment. Suspend your judgment, and imagine it is real. Imagine you could receive the body and blood of Jesus Christ under the guise of bread and wine. Imagine the Catholic experience of the Eucharist is what Jesus had in mind. Imagine how that might transform you. Imagine how receiving the Eucharist might empower you to become more perfectly the person God created you to be. Imagine how that realization would allow you to go out into the world and set it on fire. Imagine if each time we received Jesus in the Eucharist we became a little bit more of whom and what we received. Imagine . . .

There is power in the Eucharist. It is Jesus who walked the earth as our teacher—the same Jesus who died, rose from the dead, and ascended

into heaven as our Savior. It is the glorified Jesus who transcends time and space. He is the healer of my soul . . . and he yearns to be the healer of yours.

And yet, as I watch people in line for communion on Sunday, I wonder how many believe, and of those who do believe, how many take receiving Jesus alive in the Eucharist seriously. I know how easy it is for me to get distracted at that all-important moment. Even though every other moment of my week is insignificant by comparison, it still takes tremendous effort to focus on the experience.

Every age has its religious tensions, and holding my son that night, I began to reflect on how the balance of the world's major religions might change during Walter's life. The Muslim population is growing at a rate that massively outstrips

Christianity, and in my son's lifetime, Islam will almost certainly become the largest religion in the world.

This got me to thinking that if Muslims believed that Allah was truly present in their mosques, and that by some mystical power they could receive and consume him in the form of bread and wine, I suspect they would crawl over red-hot broken glass for the chance. But as Catholics, we seem so unaware of the mystery and the privilege that most of us cannot be bothered even to show up to church on Sunday.

All this certainly makes me stop and think, but deep down I am a practical man. More than twenty years ago, I developed the habit of stopping by church for a few minutes each day to sit with Jesus, present in the tabernacle, and talk about what was happening in my life. The clar-

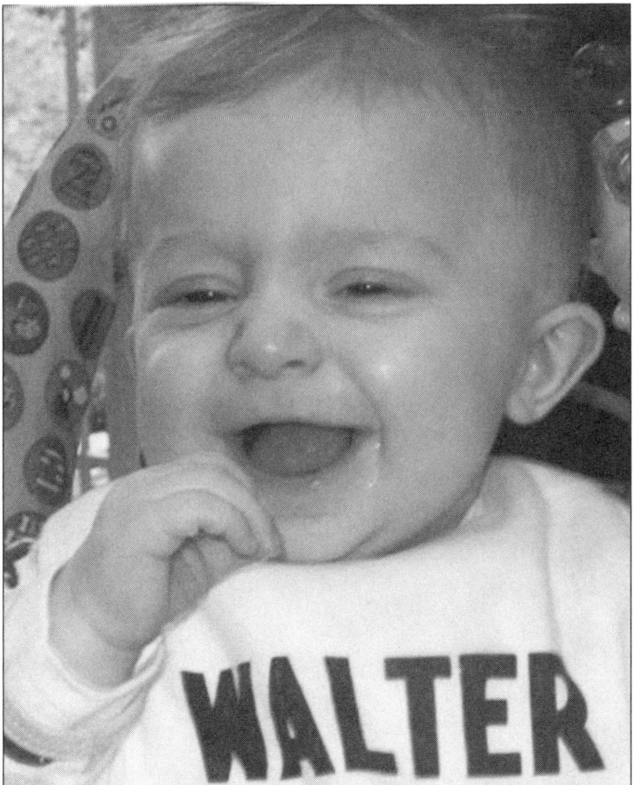
WALTER
IS THE

ity that has emerged from these conversations with Christ in the Eucharist is undeniable. Over the years I have slipped in and out of this habit. Like most people I have told myself that I can pray anywhere, but it just isn't the same. There is something powerful about his presence in the tabernacle.

Years ago, I wrote, "All the answers are in the tabernacle." With every passing year I believe this more intensely. It seems to me that we are stumbling around in the dark, blinded by our prejudices and past experiences, constantly seeking advice from the wrong people, while all the time Jesus sits waiting in the tabernacle with all the answers. What decisions are you about to make in your life? Who will you turn to for counsel?

If you have never done it, stop by your church for ten minutes every day for two weeks.

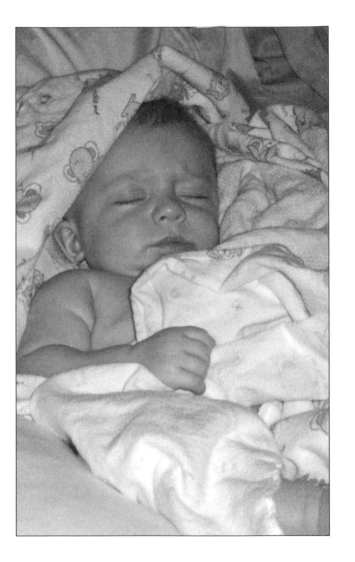

Sit as close to the tabernacle as you can. Speak to Jesus about whatever is on your mind. Or just sit there with him. After two weeks, tell me if you are not a-better-version-of-yourself. I believe you will find that you are more patient and joyful, more considerate and compassionate—more human. And to be more human is a beautiful thing.

Catholicism is a powerful humanizing force in our lives when we embrace it with humble hearts.

I hope I can teach my son to have a dynamic relationship with God. I hope I can teach him to listen to the promptings of the Holy Spirit in his life. I hope I can teach him to appreciate how powerful it is to be fed by the Eucharist. I hope I can teach him to live a life worthy of the talents God has given him. But how?

That night, sitting there, I could feel his little

self breathing against my neck, and I thought to myself, How will I teach him all these things?

It was overwhelming. But then I was reminded of a friend who had told me that the first lessons of faith come through relationships. In the care and concern I show my son, by touching him tenderly and speaking sincere words of love, I have already begun to teach him about God as a loving Father. When I go out of my way to do things for him, to help his mother, or to serve others, I am teaching him about the Eucharist, which is a powerful reminder that Jesus laid down his life for us . . . and that he calls us to lay down our lives for others.

I pray that out of all this emerges a longing to receive the Eucharist.

For three hours I sat there holding my son, and soon, I felt myself starting to dose. Getting up

WALTER P. KELLY
CEO

from the big comfortable chair, I placed him back in his crib. He sighed, rubbed his eyes a little, and rolled over without waking. As I walked downstairs I thought about the spiritual lessons fatherhood has taught me so far. Three came to mind.

God loves us. We hear this all the time in Christian circles, and for some reason I have always believed it. But now I feel it. It has become real to me in fatherhood. You see, I love my son so much. I love him more than I ever thought I was capable of loving. And if I can love him this much—with all my weakness, brokenness, and limitations—how much God must love his children.

God yearns to be with us. When I am at the office I can't wait to get home and roll around on the floor with my son, to kiss and cuddle him. When I am traveling away from home, I miss my

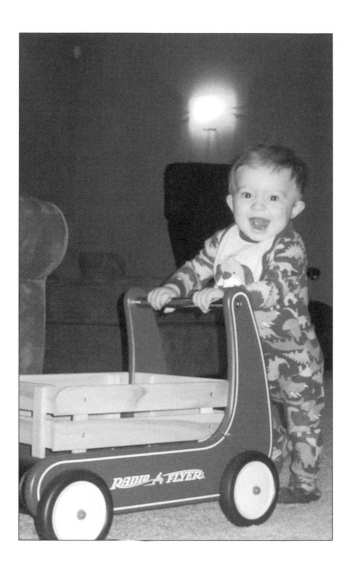

son. I miss his touch, his noises, and the sweet smell of his skin. I yearn to be with him. In the same way, as I reflect on human history and our Judeo-Christian story, what strikes me is the way that God is constantly reaching out to us. God wants to be with us. God yearns to be with us. And so often we complicate our relationship with God when more than anything else, before all the doctrines and after all the dogmas, it would seem that God simply wants to be with us.

Mother's have a unique perspective. The third spiritual insight that fatherhood has bestowed on me is that nobody sees the life of a child the way the child's mother does. I love Walter, but my wife will always have a unique perspective on his life. The only way for me to gain that perspective is to speak with her about it. And when I talk to her about her relationship with our son, it enriches not only my relationship with her, but also my relationship with Walter. If I don't talk to her about her perspective, I miss out on something of our son's life. In the same way, Mary has a unique perspective of Jesus' life, and our relationship with her enriches our relationship with Jesus.

When I reached my bedroom, I crawled quietly into bed and put my arm around my wife Meggie, who was sleeping peacefully. She is an outstanding mother and a wonderful wife. I was happy, happier than I can remember being in a long time, perhaps ever. I am a blessed man, I thought to myself . . . and I fell asleep.

## ABOUT THE AUTHOR

MATTHEW KELLY has dedicated his life to helping people and organizations become the-best-versions-of-themselves. Born in Sydney, Australia, he began speaking and writing in his late teens while he was attending business school. Since that time, more than four million people have attended his seminars and presentations in more than fifty countries.

Today he is an internationally acclaimed speaker, bestselling author, and business consultant. His books have been published in twenty-five languages, have appeared on the *New York Times*, *Wall Street Journal*, and *USA Today* bestseller lists, and have sold more than four million copies.

This title is available as a paperback edition
through the Dynamic Catholic Book Program for as
little as $2 per copy. We hope you will consider
passing out a copy to everyone who attends Mass in
your parish this Christmas.

For more information call 513-221-7700 or visit: